SCREECH! ROWF! CLOMP! RING!! AAK!
YAWN YAWN! AAK! PHOOEY RING! WHOP!
WUMP! WAAH! SMAK! BOOT! BONK! BONK! BLEAH!
BLAH! BOOT! AAUGHHH! ARF! AHCHOO! SMAK
AAUGH! AAUGH! bump! AAUGH! WHAC
SLASH! SLÜRP SMAK! SLAM! WUMP! WUMP! HAHAHAH

13 Digit ISBN: 978-1-60433-289-6
10 Digit ISBN: 1-60433-289-1

This book may be ordered by mail from the publisher. Please include $3.99 for postage and handling.

Please support your local bookseller first!

Books published by Cider Mill Press Book Publishers are available at special discounts for bulk purchases in the United States by corporations, institutions, and other organizations. For more information, please contact the publisher.

Cider Mill Press Book Publishers LLC
12 Spring Street
PO Box 454
Kennebunkport, ME 04046
Visit us on the web!
www.cidermillpress.com

Design by Jessica Disbrow Talley

Printed in China

2 3 4 5 6 7 8 9 0

# ☙ SNOOPY'S ☙
# ORGANIC DOG BISCUIT
# COOKBOOK KIT

by Snoopy
and the

**Bubba Rose**
**BISCUIT COMPANY**

ALL
RECIPES
ARE FREE OF
WHEAT, CORN
& SOY!

CIDER MILL
PRESS

BOOK
PUBLISHERS

KENNEBUNKPORT, MAINE

Artwork and Comic Strips by Charles M. Schulz

# INTRODUCTION

The Bubba Rose Biscuit Co. was founded out of our desire to give our dogs healthier treats and food. Tired of looking at long lists of preservatives and poor-quality ingredients in commercial pet food products, and with an awareness about what we eat and where it comes from, we launched the Bubba Rose Biscuit Co. and became inspired to create treats made with high-quality ingredients from food sources with names we can actually pronounce. All dogs deserve it. Honestly, a bacon treat should actually contain bacon, not a laundry list of chemicals and artificial ingredients, right? When Charlie Brown reached out to us because Snoopy needed help putting his favorite treats into a book to share with all his friends, we were happy to assist. We also thought that every dog owner and Snoopy lover deserved to have their own collection of Snoopy approved recipes that they could whip up at home for their good pups or for family and friends. Dogs do know the difference with these homemade treats, we're certain of it. So try them out. There are lots of recipes in this book to choose from, and we guarantee your dog will be happy you put forth the effort. Snoopy is!

# IT'S ORGANIC

With people spending more time and energy to find out where their food comes from and how it is made, it's natural that their focus should turn, too, to wanting to know more about what they feed their pets. My husband Eric and I are careful about what we eat and where our food comes from, which led us to do the same for our dogs, especially in light of so many large scale pet food recalls. After thoroughly researching our options, we feed our dogs a rotation diet of kibble, canned and raw food made from organic produce, and hormone and antibiotic-free meats. We use these same principles when we create the recipes that we use for our complete line of dog treats sold throughout the US and all over the world, as well as the recipes included in this book. Contrary to popular belief, Snoopy is quite the picky eater and has been requesting only organic products from Charlie Brown these days as well. Treats shouldn't just taste good, they should be as healthy and natural as a dog's regular food.

There are so many organically grown and manufactured products out there to choose from. So you should have no problem finding the best ingredients from which to make your treats. And if you do run into a problem finding an organic ingredient listed in any of these recipes, you can always swap it out for its non-organic counterpart (do try to find a quality alternative, though). Your homemade treats aren't being certified, so do your best to make them with top-notch ingredients and your dogs will love you for it. We promise!

# WHEAT, CORN & SOY FREE

Every recipe in this book is free of wheat, corn and soy – the most common sources of food allergies in dogs. We know that dogs love treats so much they'll eat them regardless of the fact that the ingredients might make them itchy or not feel well afterwards. But avoiding these ingredients and still producing healthy, tasty treats is not hard—as you'll see in our 25 recipes! By using the recipes in this book, you can take pride in knowing your dogs (and any dog to whom you give these treats) will be happier and healthier. Did you know that Snoopy was complaining about itchy skin and irritated paws before Charlie Brown started cooking him these treats, and now that he's not getting so many irritants in his diet, he's feeling a lot better and is a lot less itchy!

# THE PANTRY LIST

This is a list of the dry ingredients used most frequently in the recipes in this book. Keeping them stocked and handy will make it easy for you to bake a fresh, quality treat for your dog any day of the week. Please choose to use organic when you can. We do! And Snoopy demands it.

Oat flour
Brown rice flour
Oat bran
All-natural peanut butter
    (or peanuts to grind your own; it's easy to do)
Honey
Applesauce (unsweetened)
Wild-caught canned tuna and salmon

# STOCK THE 'FRIDGE

And the freezer too! Besides the dry ingredients listed prior, here are a few items to have on hand in your refrigerator (or to keep frozen in the freezer) so you'll have them whenever you want to make treats. As always, please choose to use organic when you can.

Shredded cheddar cheese (It saves time.)
Grated Parmesan cheese
Organic eggs
Bacon (This works especially well if you cook and drain it, then freeze it, so there is always some on hand when the mood strikes to bake homemade dog treats)
Chicken, turkey & beef
(The next time you are cooking any of these for your dinner, cook some without any seasonings or sauces, grind it in a food processor, and then freeze so you'll have the pre-cooked meat ready to use in your baking.)

Oh yeah, Snoopy is a big ice cream fan, so if you have a dog that enjoys ice cream that much too, here's a quick way to make a healthier treat for them. Just take organic yogurt bought from the store and spoon it into an ice cube tray and freeze. Then when the mood strikes, or Snoopy's banging on your door, you can pop out a cube of frozen yogurt and satisfy any pooch!

# SUBSTITUTIONS

Baking dog biscuits is not rocket science. Don't let Charlie Brown try to fool you. Things can easily be exchanged, added, or omitted, depending on what you have available or what your dog particularly likes. These recipes are all very easily adjustable. If you are making substitutions, just keep an eye on the dough consistency when mixing. If it's too dry, add more water. Too wet, add more flour. It's pretty simple. For instance, if a recipe calls for turkey, and you have chicken on hand, go for it! Or if a recipe calls for blueberries and your dog loves raspberries, swap them! Just keep an eye on the baking time. If they are browning faster than the time says, remove them from the oven. If they still look too light, add a few more minutes and keep an eye on them. Your dogs will love most things you make for them, so know they'll be happy even if you think you over- or under-cooked the treat a bit. Even Snoopy doesn't mind when his treats don't come out looking perfect, because he knows how much love and care Charlie Brown put into them.

A common substitution people email us about that's worth mentioning is the replacement of eggs in any of the recipes. All dough needs a binding agent to hold it together, we use eggs. Most dogs are fine with the one egg used in each recipe, though some dogs do have allergies to them. If your dog is allergic to eggs, here are some substitutions you can try:

1 medium to small banana = 1 egg
3 Tablespoons applesauce (use unsweetened) = 1 egg

But please keep in mind that they are not exactly the same as an egg would be, so add the liquid portion of the recipe slowly since it may take more or less due to the difference in moisture these substitutes add.

Another common substitution people look for are different flour options, either as a result of what they can find in their local store, or what they have already in their pantry. We choose to use a combination of organic oat flour and organic brown rice flour, as we tried lots of flour combinations and liked this one best, but there are lots of options. We created all our recipes to be wheat, corn and soy-free, and recommend you use a wheat-free flour if you have the opportunity, as it is such a common dog allergy these days. Here are a few other wheat-free flour choices you can use:

Amaranth flour
Arrowroot flour
Barley flour
Buckwheat flour (it's not really wheat)
Chick pea (or garbanzo bean) flour
Millet flour
Potato flour
Quinoa flour
Rye flour
Tapioca flour

# YIELDS

Most of the recipes are about the same size, so once you make one, you can anticipate how many treats you'll get out of it. Using the supplied cookie cutters, you can estimate 20-30 treats per batch and a little over one pound of treats. Enough to keep Snoopy's treat jar full for a while.

# TOOLS OF THE TRADE

The following is a list of utensils and kitchen tools used in the recipes in this book; we highly recommend them. If you don't have them, there are alternatives to use, or you can mix and stir by hand. But from experience, we can say that the easier these are to make, the better. Charlie Brown agrees!

## ROLLING PIN

They make nonstick rolling pins, which are a nice investment since you really don't want tuna in your next batch of cookies. But if you dont' have one (birthday gift list, anyone?), to prevent the dough from sticking to your rolling pin we recommend using a large plastic food-grade storage bad and placing it on top of your lightly-floured dough—then roll away. It works like a charm. A great method when baking with kids too!

## FOOD PROCESSOR

This truly is your kitchen wonder tool. You can use the grinding attachments to make your own peanut butter, chop cooked vegetables and meats down to fine pieces, etc... Once you've finished the prep work, you switch to your dough attachment and let the machine mix the dough for you. These machines are great; if you don't have one definitely drop hints to whoever might be thinking of a gift for you this holiday season. Every kitchen should have one.

## PARCHMENT PAPER

This makes clean-up a breeze. You don't want salmon in the corners of your good cookie pan, do you? If you line your normal baking pan with a sheet of parchment paper first, all you have to do is peel it off and toss it when you're done, and your pans are ready for your next batch of oatmeal cookies, Lucy's favorite!

## CUTTING MAT

We love the thin, plastic, dishwasher-safe ones. Besides cutting and prepping your food on them, they are flexible, so you can curl them and slide all your ingredients directly into the mixing bowl. Easy as 1, 2, 3.

## LATEX GLOVES

Some of the ingredients in the treats can be slightly unpleasant to work with. Who wants to mix dough with tuna in it and risk the smell permeating your hands when you work with it? Just throw on a pair of disposable latex gloves (any supermarket carries them in their cleaning aisle) and work away. When you are done, drop them in the trash and keep your hands looking and smelling the way they should.

## COOKING PANS

All the recipes in this book call for a standard flat cookie sheet or baking sheet. Any flat tray will work just fine.

# STORAGE TIPS

Remember these recipes are all for homemade, preservative-free treats. With that in mind, they can't sit out the way processed dog treats that come in cardboard boxes can. We recommend storing them in a plastic bag or container in the refrigerator. Even in there they will still mold, like your leftovers, so store only an amount you think you will use within a week. Any extras (since these recipes yield more than a week's worth of treats for most households) can be frozen to thaw out later (this works great) or given away as gifts to your friends, neighbors, coworkers or favorite beagle! Homemade dog biscuits are a great item to share and a perfect gift for the dog lovers in your life. Dogs should definitely be in on the goodness, so spread the happiness! Snoopy wants to make sure all his doggie friends are getting the same lovingly made treats that he is.

If you are looking to keep the treats on the counter, in your pocket for training, etc... and want to make sure they stay fresh for your pup, you will need to make sure you cook them nice and crispy. Thinner is better for this. If the cookies are cut thinner they will cook more quickly and get crispier, allowing them to stay fresh longer without refrigeration. Add a few more minutes to your cook time, to make sure they are crispy, and allow them to cool and air out over night, to really ensure the moisture is out of them before you move them to another container. Again, please keep in mind, we can not know what the moisture levels are in the treats you make yourself, therefore we can not tell you a specific amount of time they can maintain freshness out of the fridge, but a general rule of thumb is thinner is better, crispier is necessary, and it's safer to stay with the non-meaty recipes for this purpose.

# SOFT OR CRUNCHY?

You know your dogs and their tastes or dietary needs. If you want the treats to be softer, cook them a little less or on a lower heat (definitely keep them in the refrigerator, too). If you want your treats to be a little harder, cook them longer at a lower heat. Or, when they are finished cooking, turn the oven off but leave them in there on the tray to cool for a few hours or overnight. Remember, this is all supposed to be an easy and fun thing to do for your beloved dogs. If they don't turn out perfectly, I bet your dogs won't mind one bit and will be so happy you made something special for them anyway. I know Snoopy always is!

# RESOURCES

There are thousands of websites and books on natural canine care (how fortunate for us and our dogs!). Here are some of our favorites... Snoopy threw in some suggestions too!

*Holistic Guide for a Healthy Dog* by Wendy Volhard and Kerry L. Brown (Howell Book House/John Wiley)
*Dr. Pitcarin's New Complete Guide to Natural Health for Dogs and Cats* by Richard H. Pitcairn (Rodale)
*The Goldsteins' Wellness & Longevity Program: Natural Care for Dogs and Cats* by Robert S. Goldstein (TFH Publications)
*All You Ever Wanted to Know About Herbs for Pets* by Gregory L. Tilford and Mary Wulff-Tilford (Bowtie)

www.aspca.org
www.naturesvariety.com
www.vet.cornell.edu/library/freeresources.htm

# THE  PICK OF THE LITTER

## OUR COLLECTION OF OVER 25 OF SNOOPY'S FAVORITE RECIPES

We compiled over 25 of Snoopy's favorite recipes to create this ultimate Snoopy inspired collection for you to utilize in making wonderful homemade treats for your favorite dog, your best friends's dog, and your dog's best friend (even if he's not a famous white beagle). We hope you enjoy them! We know the dogs in your life certainly will. And if you're so inclined, we've included a few recipes for icings, in case you want to make your treats even more special or really impress your best friend. We say use your imagination and have fun with it! All of these recipes are easy and fun to make and are great projects to do with the kids.

*Note: Choose to use organic ingredients in these recipes, as we do when we make them.*

# BERRY CRUNCH

☆ PLENTY OF CRANBERRY GOODNESS IN THESE COOKIES ☆

1 $\frac{1}{2}$ c. oat flour

1 $\frac{1}{2}$ c. brown rice flour

$\frac{1}{2}$ c. dried cranberries

$\frac{1}{2}$ c. unsweetened carob chips

1 egg

$\frac{1}{2}$ c. water

Preheat oven to 350°.

Combine all ingredients (except the water) together. Add water slowly and mix until a dough forms (if too dry, add more water, too wet, add a bit more flour). Roll out on a lightly floured surface to $\frac{1}{4}$" thickness. Use a cookie cutter to cut into shapes. Line a cookie sheet with parchment paper (for easy clean up), and place the cookies on the sheet (they can be rather close together as they don't grow much while cooking).

Bake 22-27 minutes or until golden brown. Transfer and let cool completely on a wire rack. Store the cookies in an airtight container in the refrigerator. (For additional options, read the "Storage Tips" section.

# TURKEY TIME

1 $\frac{1}{2}$ c. oat flour

1 $\frac{1}{2}$ c. brown rice flour

$\frac{1}{2}$ c. sweet potato or yams (cooked)

$\frac{1}{2}$ c. ground turkey (cooked)

$\frac{1}{2}$ c. oat bran

1 egg

$\frac{1}{2}$ c. water

Preheat oven to 375°. Cook and drain the turkey, then grind in a food processor. Cook and mash the sweet potatoes (or yams).

Combine all ingredients (except the water) together. Add water slowly and mix until a dough forms (if too dry, add more water, too wet, add a bit more flour). Roll out on a lightly floured surface to $\frac{1}{4}$" thickness. Use a cookie cutter to cut into shapes. Line a cookie sheet with parchment paper (for easy clean up), and place the cookies on the sheet (they can be rather close together as they don't grow much while cooking).

Bake 22-27 minutes or until golden brown. Transfer and let cool completely on a wire rack. Store the cookies in an airtight container in the refrigerator. (For additional options, read the "Storage Tips" section.

# SNOOPY SNACKS

1 $\frac{1}{2}$ c. oat flour

1 $\frac{1}{2}$ c. brown rice flour

$\frac{1}{2}$ c. peanut butter (unsalted)

1 tsp. ground cinnamon

1 Tb. honey

1 egg

$\frac{1}{2}$ c. water

Preheat oven to 350°.

Combine all ingredients (except the water) together. Add water slowly and mix until a dough forms (if too dry, add more water, too wet, add a bit more flour). Roll out on a lightly floured surface to $\frac{1}{4}$" thickness. Use a cookie cutter to cut into shapes. Line a cookie sheet with parchment paper (for easy clean up), and place the cookies on the sheet (they can be rather close together as they don't grow much while cooking).

Bake 22-27 minutes or until golden brown. Transfer and let cool completely on a wire rack. Store the cookies in an airtight container in the refrigerator. (For additional options, read the "Storage Tips" section.

# TIDBITS

## SWEET POTATOES / YAMS

Sweet potatoes and yams are high in potassium and beta carotene (a natural antioxidant) and low in calories. They are also soothing for an upset stomach. Did you know that a tablespoon of canned or fresh sweet potatoes, yams or pumpkin on top of your dog's food will help to regulate an upset stomach?

## OATS

Oats contain a higher concentration of protein, calcium, iron, magnesium, zinc, copper, manganese, thiamin, folacin, and vitamin E than any other unfortified whole grain (such as wheat, barley, corn, etc...). They are high in fiber, amino acids, and lipids, which contain a good balance of essential fatty acids for overall good health.

## SALMON

Salmon is low in calories and saturated fat, while high in protein. It is a wonderful source of the amazingly beneficial omega-3 fatty acids, vitamin D, selenium, B vitamins, and magnesium which are excellent for skin, coat and heart health. And a great alternative protein source for dogs with allergies to the more common proteins of chicken and beef.

# PUPPY PATTIES

IT'S LIKE A LITTLE CHEESEBURGER IN EVERY BITE ✷

1 ½ c. oat flour
1 ½ c. brown rice flour
½ c. ground beef (cooked)
½ c. shredded cheddar cheese
1 egg
1 tsp. parsley
½ c. water

Preheat oven to 350°. Cook and drain the beef, then grind in a food processor. *Tip: Freeze some beef from dinner one night, before seasoning, for use in biscuits at a later time.*

Combine all ingredients (except the water) together. Add water slowly and mix until a dough forms (if too dry, add more water, too wet, add a bit more flour). Roll out on a lightly floured surface to ¼" thickness. Use a cookie cutter to cut into shapes. Line a cookie sheet with parchment paper (for easy clean up), and place the cookies on the sheet (they can be rather close together as they don't grow much while cooking).

Bake 22-27 minutes or until golden brown. Transfer and let cool completely on a wire rack. Store the cookies in an airtight container in the refrigerator. (For additional options, read the "Storage Tips" section.

# CHEESY, CHEESY!

1 ½ c. oat flour

1 ½ c. brown rice flour

½ c. shredded cheddar cheese

½ c. grated parmesan cheese

1 egg

½ c. water

Preheat oven to 350°.

Combine all ingredients (except the water) together. Add water slowly and mix until a dough forms (if too dry, add more water, too wet, add a bit more flour). Roll out on a lightly floured surface to ¼" thickness. Use a cookie cutter to cut into shapes. Line a cookie sheet with parchment paper (for easy clean up), and place the cookies on the sheet (they can be rather close together as they don't grow much while cooking).

Bake 22-27 minutes or until golden brown. Transfer and let cool completely on a wire rack. Store the cookies in an airtight container in the refrigerator. (For additional options, read the "Storage Tips" section.

# ᕔHE GREAT PUMPKIN

*✿ WHAT SNOOPY COOKBOOK WOULD THIS BE WITHOUT PUMPKIN? ✿*

1 1/2 c. oat flour
1 1/2 c. brown rice flour
1/2 tsp. ground nutmeg
1/2 tsp. ground ginger
1/2 tsp. ground cloves
1/2 c. canned pumpkin
1 egg
1/2 c. water

Preheat oven to 350°. You can also use fresh, pureed pumpkin.

Combine all ingredients (except the water) together. Add water slowly and mix until a dough forms (if too dry, add more water, too wet, add a bit more flour). Roll out on a lightly floured surface to 1/4" thickness. Use a cookie cutter to cut into shapes. Line a cookie sheet with parchment paper (for easy clean up), and place the cookies on the sheet (they can be rather close together as they don't grow much while cooking).

Bake 22-27 minutes or until golden brown. Transfer and let cool completely on a wire rack. Store the cookies in an airtight container in the refrigerator. (For additional options, read the "Storage Tips" section.

NO AFTER-DINNER SPEAKER?

# HERDER'S CHOICE

☆ THIS LAMB AND RICE TREAT IS SURE TO SATISFY ANY DOG ☆

1 $\frac{1}{2}$ c. oat flour

1 $\frac{1}{2}$ c. brown rice flour

$\frac{1}{2}$ c. ground lamb (cooked)

$\frac{1}{2}$ c. brown rice (cooked)

1 tsp. dried mint

1 egg

$\frac{1}{2}$ c. water

Preheat oven to 350°. Cook the rice and the lamb and let cool. Grind the lamb in a food processor. *Tip: Freeze some lamb from dinner one night, before seasoning, for use in biscuits later.*

Combine all ingredients (except the water) together. Add water slowly and mix until a dough forms (if too dry, add more water, too wet, add a bit more flour). Roll out on a lightly floured surface to $\frac{1}{4}$" thickness. Use a cookie cutter to cut into shapes. Line a cookie sheet with parchment paper (for easy clean up), and place the cookies on the sheet (they can be rather close together as they don't grow much while cooking).

Bake 22-27 minutes or until golden brown. Transfer and let cool completely on a wire rack. Store the cookies in an airtight container in the refrigerator. (For additional options, read the "Storage Tips" section.

# THE ELVIS

☆ BACON, PEANUT BUTTER AND BANANA TREATS FIT FOR A KING ☆

1 ½ c. oat flour
1 ½ c. brown rice flour
1 tsp. cinnamon
¼ c. banana (mashed)
¼ c. peanut butter (unsalted)
6 slices bacon (cooked)
1 egg
½ c. water

Preheat oven to 350°. Cook and drain the bacon, then grind in a food processor.

Combine all ingredients (except the water) together. Add water slowly and mix until a dough forms (if too dry, add more water, too wet, add a bit more flour). Roll out on a lightly floured surface to ¼" thickness. Use a cookie cutter to cut into shapes. Line a cookie sheet with parchment paper (for easy clean up), and place the cookies on the sheet (they can be rather close together as they don't grow much while cooking).

Bake 22-27 minutes or until golden brown. Transfer and let cool completely on a wire rack. Store the cookies in an airtight container in the refrigerator. (For additional options, read the "Storage Tips" section.

24

# PAWS IN PARADISE

☆ COCONUT IS FULL OF BENEFICIAL PROPERTIES, AND SO TASTY ☆

1 ¹/₂ c. oat flour

1 ¹/₂ c. brown rice flour

¹/₂ c. peanut butter (unsalted)

¹/₂ c. shredded coconut (unsweetened)

1 tsp. cinnamon

1 egg

¹/₂ c. water

Preheat oven to 350°.

Combine all ingredients (except the water) together. Add water slowly and mix until a dough forms (if too dry, add more water, too wet, add a bit more flour). Roll out on a lightly floured surface to ¹/₄" thickness. Use a cookie cutter to cut into shapes. Line a cookie sheet with parchment paper (for easy clean up), and place the cookies on the sheet (they can be rather close together as they don't grow much while cooking).

Bake 22-27 minutes or until golden brown. Transfer and let cool completely on a wire rack. Store the cookies in an airtight container in the refrigerator. (For additional options, read the "Storage Tips" section.

# OH, WOODSTOCK!

☆ YUMMY CHICKEN AND ROSEMARY. SORRY WOODSTOCK! ☆

1 ½ c. oat flour
1 ½ c. brown rice flour
½ c. ground chicken (cooked)
1 tsp. rosemary
1 egg
½ c. water

Preheat oven to 350°. Cook and drain the chicken, then grind in a food processor. *Tip: Freeze some chicken from dinner one night, before seasoning, for use in biscuits at a later time.*

Combine all ingredients (except the water) together. Add water slowly and mix until a dough forms (if too dry, add more water, too wet, add a bit more flour). Roll out on a lightly floured surface to ¼" thickness. Use a cookie cutter to cut into shapes. Line a cookie sheet with parchment paper (for easy clean up), and place the cookies on the sheet (they can be rather close together as they don't grow much while cooking).

Bake 22-27 minutes or until golden brown. Transfer and let cool completely on a wire rack. Store the cookies in an airtight container in the refrigerator. (For additional options, read the "Storage Tips" section.

# TIDBITS

## CRANBERRIES

Cranberries are an antioxidant rich super fruit. They are a good source of vitamin E, vitamin K, dietary fiber, vitamin C and manganese. The polyphenols, antioxidants and flavonoids in cranberries have been found to have beneficial qualities for kidney, bladder and urinary tract health, dental health and gum disease, cardiovascular health and improvements in age related declines of memory, balance and coordination in animals.

## LAMB

Lamb is a good alternative protein source for dogs who have some of the more common food allergies to chicken or beef. It is high quality protein that is rich in iron, zinc, selenium, vitamin B12, and niacin. It is lower in saturated fat than most other meat products, making it a healthy choice in your baking.

## COCONUT

Coconut is an excellent source of lauric acid, manganese, iron, phosphorus, and potassium. It is a rich protein source that supports skin and coat health. It supports healthy function of the thyroid, immune system, gastrointestinal, digestive, cell and bone function.

# SEA SNACKS

☆ TASTY AND BENEFICIAL SALMON SNACKS = SEA MEAT ☆

1 ½ c. oat flour
1 ½ c. brown rice flour
1 6-oz. can wild-caught salmon
½ c. oat bran
1 egg
½ c. water

Preheat oven to 350°. Pour entire contents of can/pouch of salmon (including all juices) into a food processor and grind.

Combine all ingredients (except the water) together. Add water slowly and mix until a dough forms (if too dry, add more water, too wet, add a bit more flour). Roll out on a lightly floured surface to ¼" thickness. Use a cookie cutter to cut into shapes. Line a cookie sheet with parchment paper (for easy clean up), and place the cookies on the sheet (they can be rather close together as they don't grow much while cooking).

Bake 22-27 minutes or until golden brown. Transfer and let cool completely on a wire rack. Store the cookies in an airtight container in the refrigerator. (For additional options, read the "Storage Tips" section.

# BLUEBERRY BITES

1 ½ c. oat flour

1 ½ c. brown rice flour

½ c. fresh blueberries (pureed)

½ c. old fashioned rolled oats

1 egg

½ c. water

Preheat oven to 350°. Puree the blueberries in a food processor.

Combine all ingredients (except the water) together. Add water slowly and mix until a dough forms (if too dry, add more water, too wet, add a bit more flour). Roll out on a lightly floured surface to ¼" thickness. Use a cookie cutter to cut into shapes. Line a cookie sheet with parchment paper (for easy clean up), and place the cookies on the sheet (they can be rather close together as they don't grow much while cooking).

Bake 22-27 minutes or until golden brown. Transfer and let cool completely on a wire rack. Store the cookies in an airtight container in the refrigerator. (For additional options, read the "Storage Tips" section.

# SECURITY BLANKET

☆ THE PUPPY VERSION OF A GRILLED CHEESE WITH BACON ☆

1 $\frac{1}{2}$ c. oat flour
1 $\frac{1}{2}$ c. brown rice flour
$\frac{1}{2}$ c. shredded cheddar cheese
6 slices bacon (cooked)
1 egg
$\frac{1}{2}$ c. water

Preheat oven to 350°. Cook and drain bacon slices, then finely grind them in a food processor. *Tip: Freeze some strips of bacon from Sunday breakfast for use in biscuits at a later time.*

Combine all ingredients (except the water) together. Add water slowly and mix until a dough forms (if too dry, add more water, too wet, add a bit more flour). Roll out on a lightly floured surface to $\frac{1}{4}$" thickness. Use a cookie cutter to cut into shapes. Line a cookie sheet with parchment paper (for easy clean up), and place the cookies on the sheet (they can be rather close together as they don't grow much while cooking).

Bake 22-27 minutes or until golden brown. Transfer and let cool completely on a wire rack. Store the cookies in an airtight container in the refrigerator. (For additional options, read the "Storage Tips" section.

# DOGHOUSE CLASSIC

☆ CAROB CHIP COOKIES, SAFE AND TASTY FOR DOGS ☆

1 $\frac{1}{2}$ c. oat flour

1 $\frac{1}{2}$ c. brown rice flour

$\frac{1}{2}$ c. unsweetened carob chips
(can NOT be substituted with chocolate)

1 tsp. vanilla

1 egg

$\frac{1}{2}$ c. water

Preheat oven to 350°.

Combine all ingredients (except the water) together. Add water slowly and mix until a dough forms (if too dry, add more water, too wet, add a bit more flour). Roll out on a lightly floured surface to $\frac{1}{4}$" thickness. Use a cookie cutter to cut into shapes. Line a cookie sheet with parchment paper (for easy clean up), and place the cookies on the sheet (they can be rather close together as they don't grow much while cooking).

Bake 22-27 minutes or until golden brown. Transfer and let cool completely on a wire rack. Store the cookies in an airtight container in the refrigerator. (For additional options, read the "Storage Tips" section.

# SLICE OF THE CITY

☆ THIN CRUST PIZZA, OF COURSE. WHO DOESN'T LOVE PIZZA! ☆

1 ½ c. oat flour

1 ½ c. brown rice flour

½ c. shredded mozzarella cheese

½ c. tomato paste

1 tsp. dried oregano

1 tsp. dried basil

1 egg

½ c. water

Preheat oven to 350°.

Combine all ingredients (except the water) together. Add water slowly and mix until a dough forms (if too dry, add more water, too wet, add a bit more flour). Roll out on a lightly floured surface to ¼" thickness. Use a cookie cutter to cut into shapes. Line a cookie sheet with parchment paper (for easy clean up), and place the cookies on the sheet (they can be rather close together as they don't grow much while cooking).

Bake 22-27 minutes or until golden brown. Transfer and let cool completely on a wire rack. Store the cookies in an airtight container in the refrigerator. (For additional options, read the "Storage Tips" section.

# ALL AMERICAN

✿ NOTHING'S MORE AMERICAN THAN APPLE PIE DOG TREATS ✿

1 1/2 c. oat flour

1 1/2 c. brown rice flour

1/2 c. applesauce (unsweetened)

1/2 c. old fashioned rolled oats

1 tsp. cinnamon

1 Tb. honey

1 egg

1/2 c. water

Preheat oven to 350°.

Combine all ingredients (except the water) together. Add water slowly and mix until a dough forms (if too dry, add more water, too wet, add a bit more flour). Roll out on a lightly floured surface to 1/4" thickness. Use a cookie cutter to cut into shapes. Line a cookie sheet with parchment paper (for easy clean up), and place the cookies on the sheet (they can be rather close together as they don't grow much while cooking).

Bake 22-27 minutes or until golden brown. Transfer and let cool completely on a wire rack. Store the cookies in an airtight container in the refrigerator. (For additional options, read the "Storage Tips" section.

# FARM HOUNDS

1 ½ c. oat flour
1 ½ c. brown rice flour
½ c. ground pork (cooked)
¼ c. applesauce (unsweetened)
1 egg
½ c. water

Preheat oven to 350°. Cook and drain pork, then finely grind in a food processor. *Tip: Freeze some pork from dinner one night, before seasoning, for use in biscuits at a later time.*

Combine all ingredients (except the water) together. Add water slowly and mix until a dough forms (if too dry, add more water, too wet, add a bit more flour). Roll out on a lightly floured surface to ¼" thickness. Use a cookie cutter to cut into shapes. Line a cookie sheet with parchment paper (for easy clean up), and place the cookies on the sheet (they can be rather close together as they don't grow much while cooking).

Bake 22-27 minutes or until golden brown. Transfer and let cool completely on a wire rack. Store the cookies in an airtight container in the refrigerator. (For additional options, read the "Storage Tips" section.

# TIDBITS

## GINGER

Ginger has a smell that instantly transforms a house into a home (just as a dog does), it is a tasty and nutritious spice. It is especially beneficial for stomach upset or delicate digestive systems. It also supports a healthy cardiovascular system by making platelets less sticky and in turn reducing circulatory problems.

## MOLASSES

Molasses is full of beneficial minerals, such as iron, copper, magnanese, magnesium, potassium, and calcium as well as vitamin B6. When purchasing molasses, choose blackstrap molasses as it contains the highest potassium levels, which help blood pressure and other cardiovascular problems.

## ROSEMARY

Rosemary is an excellent antioxidant and full of vitamin C, vitamin A, iron, folic acid, dietary fiber, and potassium. It is a natural antibiotic and antiseptic, and is known to have anti-inflammatory, anti-allergic, and anti-fungal properties. It supports immune system functions and defends against free radical damage.

# BARON BITES

1 ½ c. oat flour

1 ½ c. brown rice flour

2 tsp. ground ginger

½ tsp. cinnamon

½ tsp. ground cloves

¼ c. blackstrap molasses

¼ c. safflower oil

1 egg

½ c. water

Preheat oven to 350°.

Combine all ingredients (except the water) together. Add water slowly and mix until a dough forms (if too dry, add more water, too wet, add a bit more flour). Roll out on a lightly floured surface to ¼" thickness. Use a cookie cutter to cut into shapes. Line a cookie sheet with parchment paper (for easy clean up), and place the cookies on the sheet (they can be rather close together as they don't grow much while cooking).

Bake 22-27 minutes or until golden brown. Transfer and let cool completely on a wire rack. Store the cookies in an airtight container in the refrigerator. (For additional options, read the "Storage Tips" section.

# BEAGLE CALLS

1 ½ c. oat flour

1 ½ c. brown rice flour

½ c. ground venison (cooked)

1 tsp. ground sage

1 egg

½ c. water

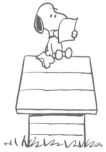

Preheat oven to 350°. Cook and drain venison, then finely grind in a food processor. *Tip: Freeze some venison from dinner one night, before seasoning, for use in biscuits at a later time.*

Combine all ingredients (except the water) together. Add water slowly and mix until a dough forms (if too dry, add more water, too wet, add a bit more flour). Roll out on a lightly floured surface to ¼" thickness. Use a cookie cutter to cut into shapes. Line a cookie sheet with parchment paper (for easy clean up), and place the cookies on the sheet (they can be rather close together as they don't grow much while cooking).

Bake 22-27 minutes or until golden brown. Transfer and let cool completely on a wire rack. Store the cookies in an airtight container in the refrigerator. (For additional options, read the "Storage Tips" section.

# SUNDAY DINNER

※ TURKEY AND POTATOES MAKE A LOVELY DOG TREAT ※

1 ¹/₂ c. oat flour
1 ¹/₂ c. potato flour
¹/₂ c. ground turkey (cooked)
1 tsp. dried rosemary
1 egg
¹/₂ c. water

Preheat oven to 350°. Cook and drain turkey, then finely grind in a food processor. *Tip: Freeze some turkey from dinner one night, before seasoning, for use in biscuits at a later time.*

Combine all ingredients (except the water) together. Add water slowly and mix until a dough forms (if too dry, add more water, too wet, add a bit more flour). Roll out on a lightly floured surface to ¹/₄" thickness. Use a cookie cutter to cut into shapes. Line a cookie sheet with parchment paper (for easy clean up), and place the cookies on the sheet (they can be rather close together as they don't grow much while cooking).

Bake 22-27 minutes or until golden brown. Transfer and let cool completely on a wire rack. Store the cookies in an airtight container in the refrigerator. (For additional options, read the "Storage Tips" section.

# GINGERBREAD IT

1 $\frac{1}{2}$ c. oat flour

1 $\frac{1}{2}$ c. brown rice flour

1 tsp. ground ginger

1 tsp. cinnamon

1 tsp. cloves

$\frac{1}{4}$ c. blackstrap molasses

$\frac{1}{4}$ c. peanut butter (unsalted)

1 egg

$\frac{1}{2}$ c. water

Preheat oven to 350°.

Combine all ingredients (except the water) together. Add water slowly and mix until a dough forms (if too dry, add more water, too wet, add a bit more flour). Roll out on a lightly floured surface to $\frac{1}{4}$" thickness. Use a cookie cutter to cut into shapes. Line a cookie sheet with parchment paper (for easy clean up), and place the cookies on the sheet (they can be rather close together as they don't grow much while cooking).

Bake 22-27 minutes or until golden brown. Transfer and let cool completely on a wire rack. Store the cookies in an airtight container in the refrigerator. (For additional options, read the "Storage Tips" section.

# SEA DOG SPECIAL

### ☆ THE DOGGIE VERSION OF A TUNA MELT, YUMMY! ☆

1 $1/2$ c. oat flour
1 $1/2$ c. potato flour
1 6-oz. can wild-caught tuna
$1/2$ c. shredded cheddar cheese
1 egg
$1/4$ c. water

Preheat oven to 350°. Pour entire contents of can of tuna (including all juices) into a food processor and grind.

Combine all ingredients (except the water) together. Add water slowly and mix until a dough forms (if too dry, add more water, too wet, add a bit more flour). Roll out on a lightly floured surface to $1/4$" thickness. Use a cookie cutter to cut into shapes. Line a cookie sheet with parchment paper (for easy clean up), and place the cookies on the sheet (they can be rather close together as they don't grow much while cooking).

Bake 22-27 minutes or until golden brown. Transfer and let cool completely on a wire rack. Store the cookies in an airtight container in the refrigerator. (For additional options, read the "Storage Tips" section.

# TACO NIGHT

1 ½ c. oat flour

1 ½ c. brown rice flour

½ c. ground beef (cooked)

½ c. shredded cheddar cheese

1 tsp. parsley

1 egg

½ c. water

Preheat oven to 350°. Cook and drain beef, then finely grind in a food processor. *Tip: Freeze some beef from dinner one night, before seasoning, for use in biscuits at a later time.*

Combine all ingredients (except the water) together. Add water slowly and mix until a dough forms (if too dry, add more water, too wet, add a bit more flour). Roll out on a lightly floured surface to ¼" thickness. Use a cookie cutter to cut into shapes. Line a cookie sheet with parchment paper (for easy clean up), and place the cookies on the sheet (they can be rather close together as they don't grow much while cooking).

Bake 22-27 minutes or until golden brown. Transfer and let cool completely on a wire rack. Store the cookies in an airtight container in the refrigerator. (For additional options, read the "Storage Tips" section.

# DOG DISH DELIGHT

☆ SNICKERDOODLES ARE A BUBBA ROSE AND SNOOPY FAV ☆

1 1/2 c. oat flour
1 1/2 c. brown rice flour
2 tsp. cinnamon
2 Tb. honey
1 tsp. vanilla
1 egg
1/2 c. water

Preheat oven to 350°.

Combine all ingredients (except the water) together. Add water slowly and mix until a dough forms (if too dry, add more water, too wet, add a bit more flour). Roll out on a lightly floured surface to 1/4" thickness. Use a cookie cutter to cut into shapes. Line a cookie sheet with parchment paper (for easy clean up), and place the cookies on the sheet (they can be rather close together as they don't grow much while cooking).

Bake 22-27 minutes or until golden brown. Transfer and let cool completely on a wire rack. Store the cookies in an airtight container in the refrigerator. (For additional options, read the "Storage Tips" section.

# BYE, BYE BIRDIE

☆ CHICKEN AND RICE TREAT GOOD FOR SENSITIVE TUMMIES ☆

1 $\frac{1}{2}$ c. oat flour

1 $\frac{1}{2}$ c. brown rice flour

$\frac{1}{2}$ c. ground chicken (cooked)

$\frac{1}{2}$ c. brown rice (cooked)

1 tsp. parsley

1 egg

$\frac{1}{2}$ c. water

Preheat oven to 350°. Cook the rice and the chicken and let cool. Grind the lamb in a food processor. *Tip: Freeze some chicken from dinner one night, before seasoning, for use in biscuits later.*

Combine all ingredients (except the water) together. Add water slowly and mix until a dough forms (if too dry, add more water, too wet, add a bit more flour). Roll out on a lightly floured surface to $\frac{1}{4}$" thickness. Use a cookie cutter to cut into shapes. Line a cookie sheet with parchment paper (for easy clean up), and place the cookies on the sheet (they can be rather close together as they don't grow much while cooking).

Bake 22-27 minutes or until golden brown. Transfer and let cool completely on a wire rack. Store the cookies in an airtight container in the refrigerator. (For additional options, read the "Storage Tips" section.

# HARD ICING

This will set and be a hard icing so you can box up the treats and give them to friends and family. You can use this on top of any of the treats in this book.

For Carob Icing (dark brown):

1 c. unsweetened carob chips
(do NOT substitute with chocolate)

For White or Colored Icing:

2 c. yogurt coating chips
Natural liquid food colorings

These chips need to be heated in a double boiler (over low heat) on the oven or in the microwave. Once soft, you can either dip your treats into them, or if you're feeling ambitious, use a pastry bag with a decorating tip to ice the tops of the cookies. If the carob or yogurt chips ar too thick to work with when melted, you can add a splash of safflower oil to help thin it out, but be careful because if you add too much it won't harden again when it cools.

Carob chips, natural food colorings and yogurt chips should be available in any health food store or the natural aisle in your local supermarket. If you are having trouble finding them, there are some great places to order them online, one such site is www.barryfarm.com

# SOFT ICING

This will be soft and require refrigeration, but is a more natural "icing," if you do not want to use the carob and yogurt chips. You can use this on top of any of the treats in this book.

1- 8 oz. package of non-fat cream cheese
2 Tb. honey
Natural liquid food colorings

Let the cream cheese warm to room temperature and then mix the cream cheese and honey in a bowl. If you want to add color, put in a few drops of a natural food coloring at this time. Spread the icing over your cookies and store in a covered container in the refrigerator.

 # TIDBIT

Carob has a taste reminiscent of sweetened cocoa, but without the theobromine, caffeine, or other psychoactive properties of cocoa (which are potentially lethal in dogs). Carob is a safe alternative for dogs. Chocolate, however, is toxic, so please never give a dog chocolate.

# ABOUT
# BUBBA ROSE BISCUIT CO.

My husband Eric and I founded the Bubba Rose Biscuit Co. in 2006 out of our desire to give our dogs healthier treats and food. Since the company's founding, we have been baking biscuits and making dogs happy from coast to coast—even overseas.

Let us introduce the test group: We have the humans, Jessica and Eric Talley (co-founders of the company and co-authors of this book) – animal lovers and rescuers since day one. Every treat we make is Human Tested, Animal Approved. And we have the pups: Bob (aka Bubba), our rescued Pit Bull and Rose (also known by her racing name of Miss Rosetta), our rescued Greyhound. They're the namesakes for the business. We now have Earl (also known as Big Fella), our rescued American Bull Dog. And gone but not forgotten, we have Weeble (or Stinky), he was our wacky little rescued Shih Tzu. He's passed on, but he's always in our hearts (ok, and tattooed on Jessica's foot). That's the gang.

Thank you for your support and for feeding your dogs the best organic treats possible. We have to get back to baking now – there are some hungry dogs waiting on us!

*Bubba Rose*
BISCUIT COMPANY

## Visit us at ❖ www.bubbarose.com

# ABOUT CIDER MILL PRESS

Good ideas ripen with time. From seed to harvest, Cider Mill Press brings fine reading, information, and entertainment together between the covers of its creatively crafted books. Our Cider Mill bears fruit twice a year, publishing a new crop of titles each spring and fall.

## Visit us on the web at:
## www.cidermillpress.com

## Or write to us at:
## 12 Port Farm Road
## Kennebunkport, Maine 04046

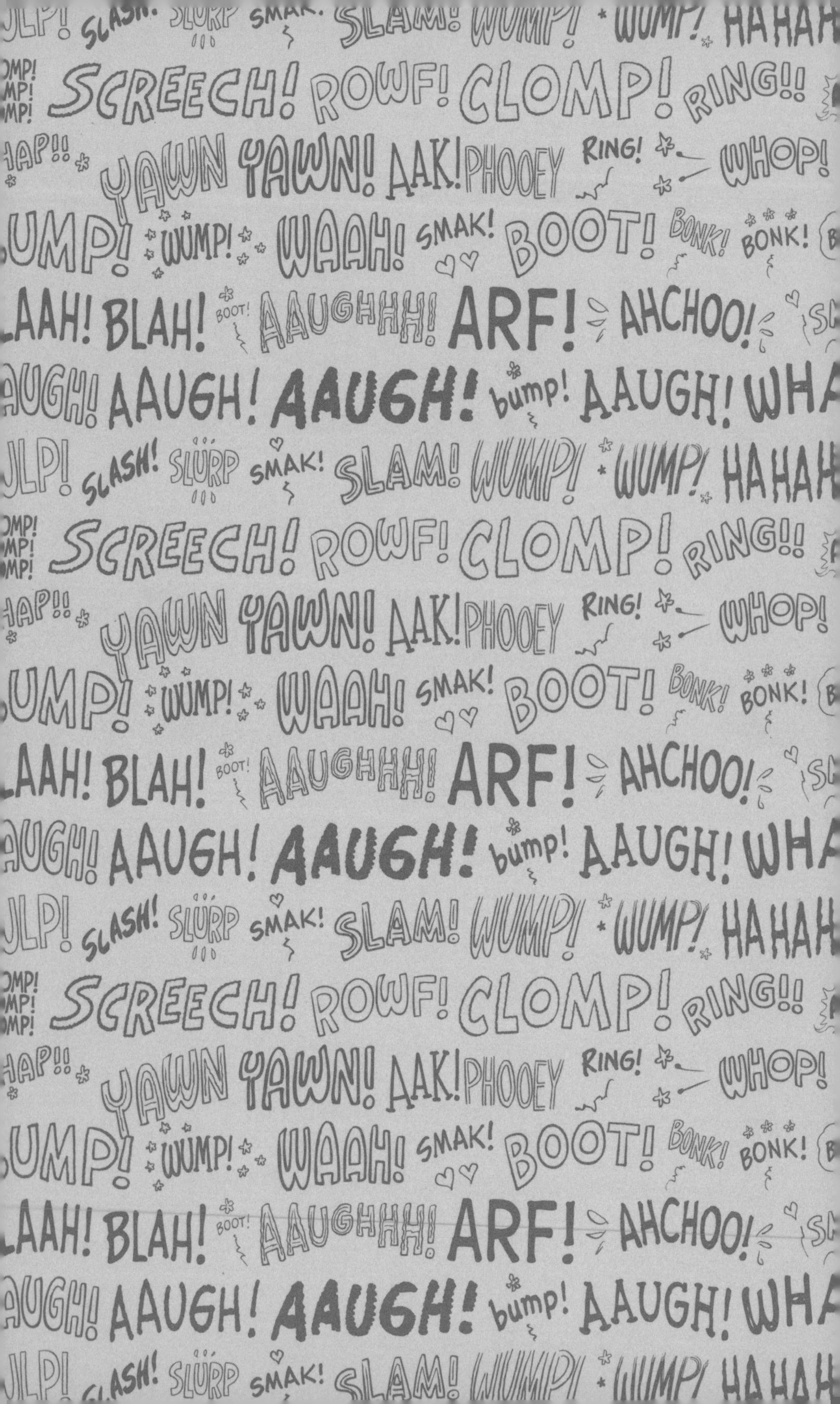